TRAMP and CAMP

By

"THE PIPELO"

Composed in Waterloo Cork, April 14th 1906

Copyright © James F Duggan – 5th November 2023

THE BOOK

Though I have written a couple of dozen books on various subjects I cannot claim to be the author of the content within this one; merely the publisher.

The wonderful writing in the manuscript, reproduced here for posterity, is entirely the work of Michael Joseph Duggan, a distant relative of mine who graced this planet with his presence around the turn of the nineteenth century.

The typed manuscript came into my possession as a consequence of a series of connections proving to me that the 'Chaos Theory' and the 'Six degrees of Separation' phenomenon have some merit in the way they influence our lives.

In re-typing this manuscript for conversion to book format I have tried faithfully to reproduce the content exactly as it was originally typed, including obvious spelling errors, irregular word spacing and dubious punctuation.

A work such as this does not deserve to be tampered with, even in the interests of correctness.

INTRODUCTION

Some years ago I received a letter, quite out of the blue, from a lovely lady by the name of Maureen Aston. She humorously claims to be only twenty-one years old, but I know she is at least half a dozen years older than me; and I am cracking on a bit. I am happy to allow her the self appointed illusion if it makes her feel better about her advancing years. She explained that she was actually a distant relation of mine whose maiden name was Duggan.

Whereas I had effectively lost contact with my Irish family relations, both near and far, she had kept in touch with them and it subsequently proved fortunate that she did so.

She had obtained my address in Birmingham from a cousin whose name was Jackie Conheady and who I had actually met some years previously when on a visit to my ancestors' homeland in West Clare, Southern Ireland. A series of correspondence ensued over the next few years whereby I was able to add, little by little, some further details to my vague family history.

However, it was only recently when I finally met her face to face that we exchanged family photographs and she tried in vain to identify who was who and educate me on my ancestry. It wasn't that I didn't care about our forbears that made her job so difficult. It was simply that I have the greatest difficulty in unravelling family trees and retaining the information; especially extended ones like ours

Now if you ask me about cosmology and the universe and want to enter into conversation on such subjects you will find me most attentive, but I still can't fix even those details in my ancient and feeble brain.

It was only very recently that she sent me a typewritten copy of a document she had referred to in earlier conversations. Judging by the text I would say it had been laboriously typed out on an ancient sit-up-and-beg Olivetti typewriter from the original handwritten script.

I began reading and couldn't put it down until I reached the last full stop. It turned out to be the recollections of the adventures in Southern Australia around the turn of the nineteenth century of a distant relative of mine by the name of Michael Joseph Duggan,

5

better known in Australia as 'Pipelo', and had been written entirely in poetic format.

It was a laborious and imaginative labour of love for a country he obviously came to have fond memories of and a document, which at the time of writing, is now 117 years old.

He was evidently an adventurous, yet soulful, man who apparently died in a far off land indirectly fighting tyranny on behalf of his adopted and much loved Australia.

I decided it was worth turning into a book. So let this be perhaps the only remaining memorial to his passing on this speck of dust in an infinitely vast universe.

RIP Pipelo.

The Manuscript

Dear reader: In this isle of ours,
Where pastures green, and emerald bowers,
And waving shrubs, and clustering flowers,
And woodlands grand,
And abbeys, forts and crumbling towers
Make fair the land

While sings the lark o'er new-sown corn,
While bursting buds the trees adorn,
While skip the bleating lambs new-born
Upon the grass,
I sit beneath a freshening thorn
An hour to pass.

The bright sun setting in the west
Each bird returning to its nest,
The oxen seeking out their rest-
In shady nooks,
And homebound labourers hardy prest
As speak their looks,

All tell us that the day is over
And that night's shadows soon will hover
O'er grass and fern, and reed and clover,
And that each stream
Will image back to many a lover
The moon's dull beam;

And when the stars peep out on high,
And people all in slumbers lie,
Visions come back of days gone by
Again to me-
Days spent beneath a sunny sky
Across the sea.

Come with me : Yes: I'll go in Rhyme
Once more into that sunny clime;
Fair land, where once upon a time
I lived and loved:
Where often to the bush-bells' chime
I sang and roved.

'Twas glorious there when toil was done
To ramble out upon the run
With my brave, noble-hearted chum-
Old Tommy Lee-
And crack a joke and turn to fun
Our misery.

Beside the lake at Purrumbete,
(Upon whose crystal waters sweet
A host of black swans - proud and neat
Does daily swim)
One night upon my usual beat
I first met him.

Together, then, for manifold
We worked until the swag we rolled,
And started off in search of gold,
-We never found-
Oh Lord' -we did get badly sold-
Tramp, tramping round.

To all the friend we bid adieu,
To cobbas, comrades, sweethearts too.
Well: what the devil could we do?
We could not stay
Our eager hearts were bursting through
To get away.

It troubled us much to have to go -
I from N - B - , you from Flo -
Our spirits they were rather low,
But very soon,
When hunger pinched, it made us know
Another tune.

Love's fancies soon were all forgot,
'Twas only on ourselves we thought,
When at a hungry shed we sought,
Some dust or stag,
We started off again with nought
In the nosebag.

Oh Lord; there are some trials out back
When tramping on a hungry track,
With nose-bag light and belly slack -
Though you've got ten -
Oh don't you think a feller'd jack
His alley in.

I can recall when Lee and I
Were starved right out - just fit to die -
How Tom looked down, then up on high
Saying "Pip where's Heaven"
"I think, old man, we'd better try
And go this even."

I answered with a sorry sigh -
"Cobba, old fellow, ere we die,
What tin we have, both you and I,
We'll go and blow'd
You know in climbing up so high
'Tmight be a load."

"Well thought" said he - so cross the plain
We struck, to make the nearest train,
And never pulled a blankey rein
Till Camperdown
We late next morn did attain -
En rought for town.

Train to Geelong, and then by boat
Across to Melbourne we did float
We had - 'think 'twas – a ten pound note
Ah'. how we flashed,
Best brand cigar and square cut coat
Till it was lashed.

Then when we found our pockets light,
And had no place to camp at night,
Says I to Lee - "What 'bout our flight
To Paradise?"
He only answered "life's too bright
To lose its joys"

And life is bright enough, God knows:
What if at times we're short of clothes:
And we are hungry: and our toes
Through our boots peep:
Too long we'll lie in the repose
Of endless sleep.

'Tis doubtlessly the fate of all-
Who've lived since our first parents' fall
For sin and ill-doings great and small
And our own pleasure-
To sip from out the cup of gall,
At our own leisure.

We toil and earn, joy and spend,
And fight and love- with foe and friend,
And sin and pray, and swear to mend
Our stubborn ways-
Until we with the dust will blend
Our crumbling clays.

Here am I lost in reverie,
Without a thought at all on Lee,
I must to find him, where is he?
My dearest Chub-
Rolling the swag- where I should be
In Holly's pub.

"Hold, Matey, just for half a minute,
Where is my tent? The Devils' in it
Tom, get my billy, run and fill it
With Jerry's beer:
Along the road, when we will swill it
Our brains 'twill clear"

Our spirits, they were rather low,
As we 'long Colac road did go:
Soon Tom hung fire, saying "Pipelo,
We'll swamp this beer,
We'll let the sneering world know
We still have cheer."

"Whenever we got funked before,
We set to work- men to the core-
And all our troubles we got O'er-
Why not to-day?
On with us once more to the fore,
Hip, hip:- hurrah:"

Mile after mile we tramped along,
Says Lee, "We soon will come out strong"
Day after day we kept agoing
Without a bob,
Until at last near Court-court- nong
We got a job.

With thankful hearts we pitched the tent,
And straight away to work we went;
We swore we'd stick to every cent
We'd earn- like wax,
To pubs, when to the town we went
We turned our backs.

And all day long we swung the axe,
Or pulled the saw with aching backs,
And mauld the wedge, and rose the stacks
All round the ship.
Lord: how we hewed like native blacks
Chip after chip.

The sun was strong, the wood was tough,
The water bad, the tucker rough,
Such things would go down bad enough
With Tommy Lee;
But he- in his most serious huff-
Would laugh at me.

And I: I'd swear and swear away
From early morn till close of day,
And then at night I'd kneel and pray-
Meaning no evil-
God to send heat and work away
Right to the Devil.

Heaven: how Lee would drive me wild
When in my own sweat I'd be boiled,
He'd say so innocent and mild,
"Pip, gi'es a song:
Throw it my honest, hearty child
The bush along"

"The bush be damned: Hell's flames and fire
May burn the bush is my desire:
An angel's patience you would tire,
A saint you'd damn,
We sing: Poor devils in the mire:
God: what a sham"

"Lee, are you serious? who could sing?
I ask you before God our king".
"Oh well - you know - I meant some thing-
Some hymn tonight"
Right 'way from me the axe I'd fling,
Laugh and recite-

THE WOOD-PUNCHER'S RHYME

I've read - I think 'twas in the bible
That God is merciful to man:
I would uphold that verse a fable:
But such would be a grievous sin.

The chips and sawdust fly around me,
I scarce can find a sniff of air,
Like furnace flames, hot winds surround me,
And scarcely leave me breath to swear

All nature seems to persecute me,
I'm pestered even by the flies,
God's mercies seem to mock and hoot me
Till I can scarce suppress the sighs.

The boiling sweat that pours like rain,
By me at times can scarce be borne,
In grief I sigh this sad refrain:-
"Alas: poor man: thou'rt made to mourn"

xxxxxxxxxxxxx ((end of wood puncher's rhyme)

"I own: I swear that's true" said Lee,
"Real picture of our misery,
But God alone can know how we
Poor devil's suffer.
Never mind - some day we'll be as free
As any duffer

"Again we'll join the favoured sort,
Again we will the town resort,
And smoke and booze, and fight and court
In street and hall.
Lord: don't we have some glorious sport
In spite of all.

"Another month and we'll be drest
In square cut coat and double vest,
And balmorals - the very best
Phit Essie makes-"
"Hold Tom and give your tongue a rest
Steady the brakes.

"You've cheered my heart right to the core,
You'll make me vain if you talk more,
"True: there are happy times in store,
For you and me.
Won't it be glorious when once more
From work we're free?

"To bid good bye to maul and wedge,
And flies and dust, aye: and the pledge,
And labour's every care and dredge,
And bush and plain,
And wear a suit of cork-screw serge
In town again.

"The very hopes of such a spell
Raise up my heart and soul as well:
-So low before they never fell
For a long time-
Come, Tom: Let's work like bloody hell
And I will rhyme."

———————————

ON THE TRACK

Here goes for to spin you a yarn:-
Well: the summer was just setting in,
Our clothes they were hellish near worn,
Our boots they were damnable thin.
I was travelling - Tom Lee, he was with me,
Six months we were roaming the track,
And although all the squatters were busy
I'd swear things were never so slack.

We travelled from station to station:
Not the ghost of a chance of a job:
Humming tucker had been our vocation,
For beer we had paid our last bob.
Ah: how often our nose bags were empty:
How often we thirsted like hell:
How often starvation did tempt me
To plunder, I cannot well tell.

Our case most deserved being lamented-
Hold hard there: no need of a laugh-
From Rokewood to Skipton we sprinted
One day, on a feed and a half.
We got there, sore footed and weary,
And camped in a hut by the creek:
Our minds they were gloomy and dreary,
Our limbs they were foundered and weak.

We seek out a plan to get labour,
We damn nearly muddled our brains:
but found ourselves further than ever
From earning our bread on the plains.
So tired of the cooks and the rations,
The flour and the Johnny-cake trade,
And cursing the squatters and stations,
Our tracks to the forest we made.

So now we are camped in South Echlin
'Tis here we have labour enough.
We are chopping dry wood for the factory:
And by —‑'s: 'tis damnable tough.
We expect getting finished by New Year,
When we mean to give labour a spell
And drown all our sorrows in good beer,
And pitch all our troubles to hell.

———————————
(end of "on the track"-

It was a week from Christmas Day,
When to Terang we made our way:
Our hearts were light, our spirits gay,
We had our rent,
In shining jimmies, straight away
From Sydney mint.

'Twas market day: In every bar
We heard the cry of " There you are-
I haven't seen you 'pon my star,
For near a year,
Where have you been, my old Jack tar?
Come: have a beer."

Beer after beer - we put them through,
Long sleeves and deep stinkers too,
Until at last a pony'd do,
We were so full.
Then Gussy spoke:- "The whole damn crew
Ought have a pull.

The Wesley Church will hold a ball
And supper - out in Echlin Hall
" We'll go there if we have to crawl
' Twill be to-night.
That's why I ask you, one and all
Not to get tight "

We all agreed that we should to,
Steve Ryan, Gus Hickey, Gar and Bow,
And the two sergeants - Bill and Joe
And Lee and I
All, when the sun was sinking low
Per coach did fly.

Round Echlin, when we did arrive,
Crowds swarmed - like bees around a hive,
And quickly through them we did drive,
And in we went.
Admission fare we would not give,
No '. Devil a cent .-

When we refused to shell the tin,
They swore they'd turn us out again,
One person hinted - 'Twas a sin
To dance and dine,
The blessed hall that night within,
'Thout paying the coin."

"You scum of hell " Joe sergeant said,
"We'll dance and dine when you'll be dead,
If you don't close your face - your head
By G— I'll break.
Do you think that we your threats do dread
You snarling snake"

Then spoke the chairman - "Trouble not
With any low-born drunken sot,
Leave them to God – He'll serve them hot
For sins like such."
Enough : We lads could stand a lot,
That was too much.

We turned the bloody place a wreck,
Joe Sergeant stretched the chairman's neck
The speaker that was up on deck
Got handled badly :
The parsons scooted from the ruck
And glided madly.

The supper - it was knocked about;
The seats and organ were thrown out;
The players and singers got the rout;
And quickly fled:
And we ? - we had a feed of stout
And cheese and bread.

We were victorious on that night,
And would again in a fair fight,
But Wesley's sons with all their might
Summoned to court;
The beggars said that black was white,
And , faith; they swore 't.

And when to us our ballots came,
Steve Ryan declared it was a shame,
And Guss and Rowson said the same
Said we should pay;
Joe Sergeant said - " In God's sweet name
I'll kneel and pray "

JOE SERGEANT'S PRAYER

" Oh Lord : thy grace I humbly ask
To aid me through the fearful task
Of fighting 'gainst the holy mask
That shrouds the faces
Of those psalm-singing curs, that bask
In Godly places.

"They preach thy works before thy face
And in some holy saintly place
They bend the knee and ask for grace,
In hopes to find it:
Lord : if you hear their mournful case,
Heed me, don't mind it.

"Oh Lord : I wish not to intrude,
And trust You will not think me rude,
When to those mongrels I allude
And tell You straightly -
The ---- debauched, or ----nude
Than them's more saintly.

"Those two-faced curs that tread Thy track
Before Thy face ; behind Thy back
Like Judas would, alas : alack :
Betray and try Thee,
And damn well swear that white is black
And crucify thee.

"They would, My Lord : I know them well,
For wordly gain they'd enter hell ;
Aye '. Even Thy holy relics sell
For worthless pelf,
Till horde on horde would help to swell
The power of self.

"They're traitors, Lord: without a doubt
And travelling on a different route
To Thine; although they preach and spout
Thy gifts and praise Thee.
Send some black plague and wipe them out
Ere they disgrace Thee.

To hell, Oh Lord : send them to bawl
Their psalms, - far – far from Echlin Hall,
Where all the devils, great and small
Shall ply around them
Brimstone and fire, till blases tall
And smoke surround them.

"Hear me, Oh Lord: You will I know,
And strike those two-faced mongrels low,
Yes : wipe them out like flakes of snow
Then, we'll be even,
And make your humble servant Joe
A saint in Heaven."

                        ------------------------(end of prayer)

Joe's prayer , I think, was but a sham,
It wasn't worth a bloody damn,
For in the court the Judge did ram
A heavy fine on:
How each looked modest as a lamb
When our case came on.

'Twas evening when we left the court,
And to the pub we did resort;
We drank some beer, and had some sport
With card and dice,
Next morn we read the law report;
'Twas flaming nice.

"Religion triumphs " the heading ran,
And this is how the case began -
"Some members of the fallen clan
Disturbed a ball
Held by the nobler race of man
In Echlin Hall.

"They turned the meeting out the door,
The banners and the flags they tore,
They raved like maniacs, cursed and swore
And looked for fight;
They swore like tigers mad for gore
That blessed night.

"they came uncalled-for to the place,
Abused John Wesley and his race;
Called Giles a smooger to his face;
McCoy a hash,
And set to work at modest pace
The Hall to smash."

And then the Wesley wowsing crew
Swore all that rotten hash was true.
And we - alas: what could we do
But hear away:
One thing was cert – the two gem two
We'd never pay.

"Be ready Tom, we'll start away
Tonight, and ere the dawn of day
The beggars - they may look for pay:
But you and I
Will be where they - search as they may
Will never try."

And he agreed, and all the rest
Resolved that they would do their best
To dodge the fine, without arrest:
"The flames of hell"
I heard then swear that they would test
Ere they would shell.

When sparkling stars peeped out on high,
And all was silent 'neath the sky,
With blueys up, Tom Lee and I
Did start away,
And many a weary mile put by
Ere dawn of day.

The swag weighed heavy on each back,
Each stomach light and nose-bag slack.
For near a week we kept the track
Through scrub and plains
While hunger, thirst and flies did rack
Our munds and frames.

We were completely fagged at last,
And almost wished this life were passed;
Remorse and misery and fast
Had told their tale
So well, what Lee wished he were cast
In hell of jail.

The seventh morn rose up to see
Us camped beneath a red-gum tree ;
Nor meat, nor dust, not tea had we
Not even a smoke,
Said I - "I cannot stick it, Lee,
My heart is broke "

"Did ever martyr here below
From fate receive so stern a blow;
Lord : before night we'll have to go
Where we'll get grub,
If not we'll find ourselves laid low
In this here scrub."

We cursed the scrub, and cursed the plain
And took the high road once again,
And when the sun was on the wane
A pub we met;
And then we tightened up our rein
Our throats to wet.

Oh, Lord : 'tis grand to sit at ease,
And munch away your bread and cheese,
And rest your weary aching knees
And quaff the pint;
And dine off mince meat, beans and peas
Or roasted joint.

To lark beneath the counter-pane
With blue- eyed Ettie, Kate or Jane,
Or walk with them by street or lane
To romp and play.
Ah: that sounds something like the grain
Of pleasure, Aye ?

To spin a yarn or crack a joke,
To lie upon a bunk and smoke
Oh : aint you then a happy bloke ?
Nor care, nor strife,
Nor stubborn interfering folk
To mar your life.

It's then you'd wish to live awhile,
When you are free from care and toil,
With plenty lubricating oil
To grease life's wheels:
When you've got slaveys for to boil
And cook your meals.

Then you would never curse the world,
With frowning brow and top lip curled
 Though many a bitter curse I've hurled
) -When on the track -
At it, or when I'd have unfurled
My sails out back.

Though many were the joys we met,
We blokes enjoyed them all, you bet
How we'd lay back our ears, and get
To work with minds,
When e'er the table would be set
With meat or viands.

One week of such you well may know
Repays us for an age of woe :
The world may bump me thro' and fro,
And down and up,
My motto is, where'er I go -
"SMOKE , DINE and SUP ."

A life of change is being mine.
Sometimes I drink the choicest wine,
And off the choicest meats I dine -
At times I thirst,
And starve, and for tobacco whine,
- A kind of curst –

But yet ; in spite of all life's sorrow
It's sad today and feared to-morrow.
The few short days of joy we borrow
Out weighs the strife,
And make us stick onto the narrow,
Rough road of life.

Tom Lee and I kept going like earls,
Boosing and making love to girls,
That wore false teeth and falser curls,
To lure our tin.
A shanty pub in this here world's
A devil's den.

How shanties take the tin away
You'd scarce believe, until you'd pay
Your bills, and have to start away
' gain on the track:
With Bluey ,milldewy and gray,
Strapped on your back.

Again we had to tramp away,
One dazzling, sunny, summer's day:
Yet we were happy, free and gay
And fit for toil:
Behind were laws and fines to pay :
Two hundred mile.

Christmas about a month was gone
And ballast work was coming on:
We knew a ganger - Sandy Don -
We sought him out,
And good enough, he signed us on,
To pick the grout.

'Twas glorious work - the scran was good,
A man can work when he gets food.
The wages were a bob a load -
And train fare free,
We swore we'd gravel all the road
Without a spree.

We toiled away; and when 'twas done
We saw the light of April's sun,
And got a job upon a run
Quite close to hand:
The owner was a convict's son
From Tassey land.

'Twas when the gold fever was high,
His father did the station buy:
He owned all that the keenest eye
Could see across.
Twas his from Warrior Hill so high
To Beeac Cross.

And when the old man died, the son
Became the owner of the run,
And he was muchly given to fun
And maidens fair
He was a reckless sort of gun -
A devil – may – care.

He was a sport, and many a race
He won by nags bred on his place;
He owned a pack; joined in the chase,
And polo played.
Went headlong at the devil's pace
But always paid.

It was a pleasure working there;
The labour light; the wages fare;
The manager : I do declare
I'd call him "Dear"
And when we had a pound to spare
The "Gums" was near.

The "Gums", it was a shanty, and
The stuff sold there was simply grand:
'Twas made by the proprietor's hand
- He called it wine -
From grapes that grew upon the land,
'Twould kill a swine.

It's there you'd meet a wholesome band,
The brightest boys in all the land,
Men of all creeds - from every strand
and race in life:
Yet, all were comrades, heart and hand,
In peace and strife.

You'd hear some noble stories there,
Right up on end they'd make your hair
Stand stiffly, and your eyeballs stare,
And lower jaw drop
So ghastly, terrible and queer,
They'd turn your top.

There, in the cellar, many a night
We drank the wine, both red and white,
Until the morning's dazzling light
Shone from above
And then, we'd get to work - or try it-
Scarce fit to move.

Joe Boyce, Carew and Jack Devine
And the O'Mearas, Mick and Brian
The Brennans three and Jerry Ryan
And Arthur Wright
Like stars amongst the rest did shine
So sweet and bright.

They were a wild and reckless sort,
O'erflowing with mischief, fun and sport,
When they the shanty would resort,
They'd make things hum.
You'd think the devil with his court
To earth had come.

In this here world they had no care,
But eat enough and drink and swear,
Whenever they'd a quid to spare
They'd go and spend it;
And if a feller acted square
They'd gladly lend it.

They'd treat a man as he'd deserve,
Their open hearts and iron nerve
From honest ways would never swerve,
No : - never a bit;
This sleping world, may Heaven preserve
Such men in it.

How dearly they did prize a joke :
Aye : just as much as beer or smoke:
Dare devils : half the local folk
Would shake with fear,
Whenever any reckless bloke
Of these was near.

They'd swap the farmer's nags at night
And put them in a sorry plight,
And cause them many a bloody riot,
Lord : what a sham
To see the devils tare and fight,
And curse and damn.

One night within the shanty, we
Were all a bit heavy on the spree;
The pipes were pulling glorious free
The lamps did shine:
And full of joy and mirth and glee
We swamped the wine.

The stories were as usual told,
'Bout highwaymen and mines of gold;
How peppered claims were bought and sold,
And piles were made.
And one-time heroes brave and bold;
Now in the shade.

Bob Martin spat upon the floor,
And called Fred Brennan to the fore,
And asked him for to tell once more
The minstrel joke.
Fred on a log, sat near the door -
He smiled and spoke.

"I guess this story is not new,
To any blasted one of you.
You all have heard what happened to
The Ladies' men
But anyway, as it is true,
I'll tell it 'gain."

" THE HANLEY AND WILLIAMSON JOKE"

Bawly Williamson and Jimmy Hanley,
You all must have heard of their names.
They are kind and polite to the ladies,
And up to all love-making games.
They are modest and courteous and civil;
Yet sneaking and cunning and sly
And they care not for God or the devil
When a young lady winks them an eye.

No matter a damn how much ladies
Would be at a party or ball
These two bare-faced youths I have mentioned
Had their pick and their choice of them all.
Were they men : then it would not surprise me
But, Lord : they were only mere lads,
Who instead of love making to ladies
Should stop quietly at home with their das

Well, the rest of the boys could not stand it
They plotted night, morning and noon
For a way that would turn their whistle
To play them a different tune.
So it happened that down in the Warrions
They started a minstrel troop,
And they got these two love-stricken fellows
To form a part of the group.

They made them to represent niggers,
They painted their faces with cork,
Till they looked both in form and in figures
Like two black waiters found in the York.
Then they went through their drill and their practice
Till each one could master his part;
Till they knew all their gags and quick answers,
And knew all their rhyms off by heart.

The niggers were regular boshters;
They painted for practice each night,
Till at last all the waves in the ocean
Could not wash their confounded cheeks white,
Then they painted damn great advertisements
On factories, bridges and trees.
The words I can't think of exactly,
But, I think, they ran something like these.

"The minstrel troop from the Warrions
Will hold at the Coreroke Hall
A concert - admission a shilling -
And after the concert a ball ".
Well : the night came around for the concert
The hall, it was packed to the door,
And the wit of the newly-fledged minstrels
Caused many a merry uproar.

And as soon as the concert was over
And the hall was cleared out for the dance,
The fate of the lady-struck minstrels
Could be easily seen at a glance.
For the paint they had used on their features
Left a dirty brown shade on their brows;
And , in spite of all washing and scrubbing,
They looked like a pair of starved chows.

Their cake it was dough with the ladies,
Who could not stand China-man stink;
How the rest of the boys in the Warrions
Will tell you the tale with a wink:
Yes - over and over they'll tell it,
While they sit in the cellar and smoke;
And the name that they call their adventure
Is "The Hanley and Williamson Joke ".

(End of Joke)

So rolled the tide of time away,
As varied as my foolish lay;
Until at last there came a day -
A day of pain -
Tom Lee resolved to go away
Across the main.

He broke the news, saying - "Pip, old boy,
'Twill cost me many a weary sigh,
But never mind, I'm going to try
New Zealand's shore.
'Tis said that in its gullies lies
The shining ore."

"'Tis sad" he said "from Vic. to part"
(here did I see the bright tear start)
He mastered it with noble heart,
Then forced a smile,
"And leave The Land of Toby Bart
For Seddon's Isls".

"But things are gone to hell of late,
Here in this federated state.
Ruin's coming at a headlong rate
To smite us all -
We'd better scoot ere it's too late
And we should fall.

"The Cockey's mortgaged in the bank,
The squatter's herds are growing lank,
The mills and sheds are getting rank,
The government
Is getting weak around the flank
'Taint worth a cent.

"What little cash we earn here
Would never keep a man in beer,
And we will earn less next year-
If we don't go,
We'd better start for Melbourne pier
Eh : Pipelo:"

"Tom" I replied, "You're talking straight
Your question will not bear debate,
'Tis true, the weather, time and State
And work and pay
Are sinking at the devil's rate
Into decay.

"Yes every day is getting worse,
As if some devastating curse
Were hurled with most infernal force,
By some vile hand,
To drain man's life-blood and his purse,
And burn the land.

"We're grafting here from day to day,
And scarcely earn enough to pay
To keep our souls housed in their clay
'Tis simply hell -
I think the best and wisest way
'S to give it a spell.

"But yet 'tis scarcely worth my while
To steer my barque to 'Seddon's Isle',
I'll weather out another while
Upon this shore,
And then back to the Emerald soil
I'll go once more.

"And you : of course you may be right,
To spread your wings and take your flight,
And on some other shore alight -
Some shore less dear,
Where in man's prospects are more bright
And fair than here.

"Please suit yourself, dear honest Lee,
I trust you won't consider me:
Though we had many a tramp and spree
And fight together,
We'll part some day - that's fate's decree -
Each from the other"

" 'Tis true " he answered with a sigh,
"For three long years, both you and I
Have tramped and worked, through grief and joy,
Each with a heart:
And now the hour is drawing nigh
That we must part.

" I will: yes Pip: I will away :
The good ship's anchored in the bay,
Tomorrow at the close of day
She'll bear me off.
And you?" "I'll see you on your way"
"Pip, you're a toff"

'Thout more ado we drew our tin,
And soon were settled down within
A railway train, and off did spin
To Melbourne town.
The midnight hou was chiming when
We landed down.

It was a splendid summer's night,
The City lamps shone clear and bright,
It was indeed a glorious sight,
So dazzling fair,
It would the saddest heart delight
And banish care.

The poor and humble, rich and proud,
All mingled in one common crowd:
The rush and bustle, noise and loud
Tramp, tramp of feet
As on we shouldered, squeezed and ploughed
Through lane and street

Through crowds of lady folk and men,
Through streets of fashion, lanes of sin:
Past many a brothel, slum and den
We pushed our way
Until at last we sttod within
"The Dawn O'Day".

The "Dawn O'Day" is an hotel,
Wherein you'll get a glimpse of hell:
- The larriken and broken swell,
In it are met
And there they drink and swear and yell
And game and bet.

The Dagoes and the Japanese
The Chinamen and Portuguese
The Swedes and Turks and Bengalese,
In it are found:
They come from over all the seas
The world around.

I'll say, for truth, it is a place
Where you'll find men of every race:
All steeped, nay -buried in disgrace
And sin and evil:
Each one has written on his face
The one word – "Devil"

Matey and I went for a look;
We saw enough to fill a book
'Twould do you good to have a cook
In there some night;
You'd wonder how Old Nick could hook
Such angels bright.

And Oh: - The ladies that are there :
Their very breath pollutes the air:
Sore eyes, dull cheeks and waving hair
Of fairest shades
Fall o'er their necks and shoulders bare
In shining braids.

Oh: who would think that any maid
Could ever fall to such a grade:
Fall down till even the faintest shade
Of virtue flew
And self -respect to them has bade
A long adieu.

Masses of vilest sin are they,
Mere moving heaps of putrid clay.
Of hope for them the faintest ray
Does never shine:
They booze and smoke and live away
In shame and crime.

They mix with every race and creed,
The Pigtail , German ,Turk and Swede;
They do not mind what kind of breed
They will embrace;
Australia owes to them, indeed,
Her pie-bald race.

Well, we were at the "Dawn O'Day"
We drank and looked on many a play,
The dice were thrown upon a tray,
The slips went round:
Some spielers, playing at banker, lay
Upon the ground.

All things were running smooth and well,
When suddenly I heard a yell -
"Confound your soul : You scum of hell
You German hog :
Put back that card, or else I'll shell
Your brains you dog."

That was enough to start a fight;
Glasses and chairs flew left and right,
And soon there was a gruesome sight
At "Dawn O'Day"
The devils kicked up hell's delight)
We ran away.

'Twas nearly day; We walked about
The streets, until the sun shone out,
And then we took the shortest route
To Cohan's Pub,
And there we had a good blow -out
Of finest grub.

We knocked about the town all day,
When evening came we took our way,
Unto the docks where ready lay
The good ship grand;
That soon would bear poor Lee away
To Seddon Land.

'Bout seven O'clock she wheeled to sea
I bid good-bye to Tommy Lee:
Oh : never, never more we'll spree
Or fight together:
Or camp beneath a shady tree,
In burning weather.

FAREWELL TO LEE

Farewell, dear Lee: a long farewell
Though sorrows may be mine,
Though I may feel the pangs of hell
May cares be never thine.

May plenty always on thee smile,
May friends be true to thee.
Thou wert an honest son of toil
And, thou wert true to me.

Go where I will, I ne'er will find
Another mate like thee;
So noble and so true of mind
So generous and so free.

Through weary life we many a day
Together pulled along;
Whenever sadness dimmed our way -
We cheered it with a song.

We worked and earned, boozed and spent
We lead a careless life:
We feasted, borrowed, starved and lent,
Through pleasure and through strife.

We tasted life in every form -
The bitter and the sweet
We weathered many a shaking storm,
In bush as well as street.

But care, nor strife, nor angry brawl,
In bush or plain or town,
Could ever get us to the wall,
Or break our spirits down.

Dear Tom, 'twas sweet in days gone by,
When wearied out with toil
To sit beneath a starry sky
And watch the billy boil.

'Twas sweet to lie upon the grass,
Free from all wordly care,
And watch the smoke-clouds as they'd pass,
And mingle with the air.

Those days have gone: Those joys have fled.
All, all have passed away;
My weary heart weighs down like lead
- Would I were only clay:

Farewell to every hope and joy:
- Oh cold : Oh, stern fate:
Farewell : Farewell: dear honest boy:
A long farewell : dear mate-

Alone:: without a mate or home,
Once more I to the bush did roam;
And when beneath the starry dome
I'd camp to rest
Sweet thought of matey o'er the foam
Would fill my breast.

Resolved at last to rest my feet,
I took the train to Purrumbate,
Truth is - I kind of thought I'd meet
N - B - there
But soon I found she did a skete
Some other where.

Jim Turner asked - "Where have you been"
Why man, 'tis ages since I've seen
You, J--- 's Pip, you have got lean,
And where's Lee?"
"Jimmie" said I "the sea's between
Poor Tom and thee."

I told him all that happened then,
Sincewhere my story did begin;
'Bout how we worked and earned tin,
And knocked it down,
In booth, and grogshop, pub and inn,
In bush and town.

Yes: all out wild and gay career,
I told him as I've told it here.
He was a comrade sincere
That I could trust -
And was not shy to shout a beer,
When he'd havedust.

And when at last my store ran out
"Come Jim" said I "tell me about
This place; For there can be no doubt
There's many a change
'Bout here, since Lee and I struck out
The bush to range.

"say'. how are all the girls so dear?
And how are all the coves round here?
Ah'. some of them are gone I fear,
Married or dead".
He kind of coughed - his pipes to clear;
Then up and said -

"Yes: Pip : there have been chages many
Fat Sal is wed, and little annie
Has done a guy - she did it cannie -
She left no trail.
Fred Lane has flown and left poor Fanny
To weep and wail.

" And Jessie left a baby boy,
Her ashes in the churchyard lie.
And Gertied Beach has gone to try
The opera stage,
Poor Elsie Wynne went on the sly
And wed Jack Page.

"Sweet Flora's waiting as you'll see
For the return of Tommy Lee;
N-- B---'s as true as gold to thee -
Now Pip : don't frown;
She's gone from here - I think that she's
In Camperdown.

"'Tis but a month till Boxing Day,
'Taint worth your whild to go away.
Things will I know be hellish gay -
(Wine , Ale and beer)
There'll be a picnic o'er the way;
N – will be there

"well Jim " I said "I can't remain
There is a job on Pitfield plain,
They're going to metal ninety chain
Of wagon track
But, Boxing Day, as sure as rain
I will come back"

And sure enough on Boxing Day
I to the picnic made my way
Oh Lor: we had some glorious play -
I met her there -
Expenses ran a fortnight's pay,
What did I care?

Music and dancing, beer and wine;
'Twas grand : 'twas splendid ':: 'twas divine:::
Banished was every care of mine
My heart was light;
But oh: things were not half so fine
Going back that night.

I went with Turner to "Lake View"
His girl and mine came with us too.
Oh Lord: how quick the moments flow
You couldn't know.
At ten o'clock I said "HursO:
I've got to go"

My camp was sixty miles away,
The road through scrub and barriers lay,
And I should bike it before day -
I should be back
To meet the seven a.m. hurray,
Or get the sack.

The very thought that I should start
Went through me like a poisened dart,
A coldness crept around my heart
My soul did move;
Ah : 'tis very hard to part
From those we love.

And so I bid my girl good-bye,
Poor N---, I saw her vainly try
To smother back each heavy sigh
That left her heart -
I saw the tear-drop in her eye
Refuse to start.

How little did I dream that night -
Whilst gazing on those orbs of light
That shone so beautiful and bright
Above a face
Which would an artist's soul delight;
His studio grace -

That never more upon my breast,
My N---'s head would lay to rest;
Nor never more (her sweet lips prest
Close to my ear)
I'd hear her vows of love confess,
So fond and dear.

'Tis years ago, yet never trace
I've seen since then of N---'s sweet face;
But time or distance can't efface
From out my mink
A gentle form - and soul of grace -
So pure and kind

Well : to my tale - Jim shook a flip,
And said "Good-bye, my dear old Pip.
Here take this flask,you'll want a nip
Ere you arrive;
And when you'll land just mail's a slip
That you're alive"

"I will " said I, then did a guy,
And on the wheels away did fly:
And what befell me bye-and-bye -
If you would know -
Just rub the cob-webs from your eye
And look below.

Yes down below, the note I wrote
To Turner; I for you will quote.
What sorrows did befall the poet
In it you'll fine;
That it is true as gospel know't
And bear't in mind,

TO J. TURNER

Dear Jim, with pen and ink here goes
To tell you plainly all the woes,
That round me on all sides have rose
Since I left you,
And they are numerous - God knows-
And bitter too.

I paddles on to Pomberneit,
As quick as I could spin my feet;
I stuck like wax upon the seat,
- I rode quite game-
'Twas down the rough and ridgey beat
My troubles came.

The morn was just about to rise,
I saw her light spread 'neath the skies;
Thoght I - well this is Paradise;
There's nought so fine
The road stretched out before my eyes
A shining line.

And as the moon rose higher and higher
So rose my hopes - until the fire
Of Fame had kindled a desire
For record riding;
Then faster, faster whirled the tyre
Down hill and siding.

The trees and barriers dropped behind,
Lord; I was riding like the wind;
At least I thought so, in my mind;
But pride must fall,
The blankety moon right up behind
A cloud did crawl.

Death's gashtly terrors filled my soul;
The bike was gone from all control;
Where will she pitch me? in a hole,
Or 'mongst the rocks?
Where living creatures never stroll
Except the fox.

On must I go : -bon gre: mon gre
The devil a barrier could I see;
Nor fence, nor rock, nor scrub nor tree
By G--, 'twas dark.
Thought I,"this ride will finish me
'Twill quench my spark"

I said 'nough prayers to fill a book,
I cursed and damned my stinking luck,
And straightway then the gigger struck
On Dunfords dog -
He turned the steering wheel amuck
Into a log.

I went a header then and there,
And shot like lighting though the air,
I found a resting, fair and square
Inside the fence;
The logs and rocks lay everywhere
The scrub was dense.

A mangled heap of flesh and bone,
Lay huddled up against a stone;
And many a mournful sigh and groan
Went to the sky,
From me -Whilst I lay there alone;
None heard me sigh.

Cuts, scars and wounds from hat to boots,
My hair all torn out from the roots;
And worse than all - my Sunday suit
Was ripped and torn;
I never suffered so acute
Since I was born.

I felt that death was hovering near;
I raised my head and wiped a tear;
Then offered up a prayer sincere
To God our King,
That he would bear me to the sphere
Where angels sing.

But it seems I wasn't fit to go,
Just then from out this world of woe.
Death did not want me : Did he? No:
He did not care
To carry off poor 'Pipelo'
To his last lair :

When that I saw, hope filled my heart,
Thought I - I'll make another start,
And from this deathlike scene depart
And onward plod.
But Lord the bike aint worth a ----
So help me God.

Her "gib" got tangled in a spoke;
Her fore and stern wheels were broke;
Her rudder ruptured - 'twould provoke
A saint to madness.
I filled my pipe and had a smoke
To soothe my sadness.

Then set to work in all my haste,
To fix the tyres with patch and paste;
In all my days I never faced
A job so tough.
I'd blankey little stuff to waste
I'd scarce enough.

I rectified her joints and steerings,
I screwed her nuts and oiled her bearings;
I pumped her bladders, greased her gearing ,
Then rode away.
I noticed that the sky was clearing,
'Twas nearly day.

The sun was shining high and bright
When Pyrion-Yalloak hove in sight;
"My luck was in " said I - "I'm right,
I'll pull up here,
And drown the sorrows of the night
In cosey's beer".

Well - there I stopped till close of day,
Then to the camp I pegged away;
And wasn't there the devil to play;
The boss was mad:
"Come here" he roared " and get your pay
You drunken cad".

"Right oh" quoth I, and over I went
Across the paddock to his tent:
And ther e he counted out my rent
Some five score bob;
And I : well, sure, I took the hint
And left the job.

So now once more, I'm on the track,
With bluey strapped across my back,
And things are so confounded slack
I've got no show -
My prospects never seemed so black,
My cake is dough.

Bit Lord: I swear by earth and sky,
And by the sun and moon so high,
That if again I do come by
Another job
I'll stick to it until I die,
So help me bob:

18m damn well sick of travelling o'er
The track so often trod before;
So I'm resolved to roam no more -
I'll do a spell,
Until my spirit quits this shore
For Heaven of Hell.

Well Jim, I think I'll say adieu,
With best respects and love to you,
And all the friends and comrades true
In Purrumbete.
I hope the days will be but few
Until we meet.

Write soon; I'm waiting a reply,
I'd like to hear from you old boy
There's nought would give me greater joy,
- As you might know -
Till then, old man, Ta-Ta : Goodbye:
Yours Pipelo"

Whiles working and whiles knocking round
Time fled, until at last I found
Myself 'board steamer homeward bound;
Good old Geelong:
Your masts and spars are firm and sound
Your ribs are strong.

One night when all were fast asleep,
I to the topmost deck did creep,
And sung unto the briny deep
My farewell song;
As fastly o'er the seas did sweep
Our ship along.

FAREWELL TO AUSTRALIA

Farewell : a long farewell, beloved land :
Perhaps no more thy beautious shore I'll see,
But wheresoe'er I roam thy scenery grand
In memory's wings will oft come back to me.

Thy wild romantic scenery I love,
Thy mountains, hills and gullies I adore.
Sad fate to think that I no more may rove
Amidst those scenes where oft I roamed before.

Dear, dear to me is my own native home:
And dear the friends my early childhood knew
But yet: while sailing to them o'er the foam
A pensive yearning binds my soul to you.

As o'er the dark blue sea our good ship steams
My every thought doth wonder back to thee;
For on thy land all nature's blessings teams
And thow dost hold much that is dear to me.

For oh: the girl, the girl thatI love best,
Doth live beneath the splendour of thy skies.
Farewell: Oh heaven 'twill burst my aching breast
To think she's lost for ever from mine eyes.

Oh cruel world: I dread your bitter ways.
I care not now how soon I fill the grave,
My lamp of life has lost its brilliant rays
Since I to roaming thoughts became a slave.

I cannot quiet the restlessness of soul,
That drives me headlong to my bitter doom.
On must I travel - heedless of the goal -
Until my ashes moulder in the tomb.

Then once again farewell beloved shore:
Farewell: may every blessing on thee shower,
May health and peace and plenty long reign o'er
Thy every hill and valley, shrub and flower.

May all thy sons and daughters live in joy,
And no false notions break contentment's spell;
On them may God smile from His throne on high:
Farewell : farewell: a long last fond FAREWELL

AFTERWARDS

Well now, I think I'll have a pull,
My bit of brain is gathering wool,
I only menat to stop an hour
When I sat down beneath this bower
And now 'tis very nearly day
And all the night I've raved away.

No wonder people say I'm mad,
And no one wonders that I'm sad.
I, by the Lord, for this will sorrow
Cold teethaches and the P --- to-morrow.
Dear reader - I will say Goodbye
And scoot away to lullaby.

THE END

Dear Reader,
      Kindly breathe a little prayer for the writer, M. Joe D
(known in Australia as Pipelo) who was reported missing in
Messopot on 7th July 1917, and not since heard of. Presumed
dead.
May he rest in peace.
F.E.D.
2nd June 1930

Publisher's Post Script.

I am now going to try, with some difficulty, to unravel and clarify the last entry headed 'Dear reader'.

From discussions I have had with my cousin Maureen Aston, (nee Duggan) referred to in the introduction, I have reason to believe that had the page been wide enough to accommodate the type-setting, 'M. Joe D' should read 'M Joseph Duggan' (the 'M' being Michael) and likewise ' Messopot' should read Mesopotamia, now more commonly known as Iraq.

It is unknown who or what the initials F.E.D. represent. The only possible connection I can find is Francis Edward Duggan (1883 – 1956) whose name according to a genealogy search pops up fairly close to a Maurish Duggan. As the dates infer he may have had some personal and direct knowledge of the author. However, the connection is tenuous and as such they will have to remain a mystery.

According to Maureen the date '2nd June 1930' is believed to be when this copy of the manuscript was laboriously set to type by the said Maurish Duggan, another distant relative.

Maureen is of the opinion that when Joe Duggan (known as Pipelo in Australia) returned to Ireland from his adventures in southern Australia he joined the British army. He was subsequently shipped out to Mesopotamia where he was reportedly thought to have been killed in action around the 7th July 1917; though there is no confirmation of this and an initial search of military records has proved fruitless. However, subsequent information seems to indicate that the report was confirmed on 3rd October of that same year.

Final note:-

Michael Joseph Duggan, Born 1878. (known as 'Pipelo').
Emigrated to Australia 1898, aged 20.
Returned to Southern Ireland 1906.
Moved to England 1907.
Joined British army. (date unknown).
Died Mesopotamia, 7th July 1917. (details unknown).

Acknowledgments

The image used on the front cover of this book was painted by Herbert Buckmaster who, as you can see, was a very talented painter of Australian heritage.

This and many of his other works can be found in the National Gallery of Victoria in Australia. A Google search will soon find them.

I came across this image purely by chance and decided there and then it should grace the cover of this book. There were two reasons for this.

The first is that the scene conjures up in the mind's eye exactly the type of existence the author of this manuscript, Michael Joseph Duggan (Pipelo), must have experienced as he narrates it during his eight year stay in Australia. It rather proves the saying 'a picture is worth a thousand words'.

Secondly, the fictional man depicted by Buckmaster is the spitting image of a cousin of mine named Joseph Conheady who the artist could not possibly have ever met. Is that weird or what? It caught my eye and I just had to use it.

James Duggan.

Mea Culpa.

Due entirely to my previously stated feeble brain and its inability to recall accurately discussions held in the past it is possible that some of the supporting information contained herein could be incorrect. If this proves to be so then I sincerely apologise and stand to be corrected.

If anyone wishes to enlighten me or even add to the narrative I will be happy to make the necessary corrections and republish accordingly.

I may be contacted at the following Email address.

jimduggan@supanet.com

THE LYRICS OF LIFE

This is a book of 53 verses containing up to a dozen stanzas each. It reflects the author's perception of life with all its idiosyncrasies. Some are humorous; others are of a more serious nature. All are well observed manifestations of life.

RHYME AND REASON

This is a book of 30 verses containing up to a dozen stanzas each with supporting descriptions of their content. It reflects the author's perception of life with all its idiosyncrasies. Some are humorous; others are of a more serious nature. All are well observed manifestations of life.

THE POETRY OF THE UNIVERSE

This book presents a unique and interesting introduction to the wonders of the known universe. It is written almost entirely in the form of verse and supported by colour images and notes for those who may wish to delve a little deeper. It is a reflection of nearly sixty years of observation by the author and his perception and interpretation of all things universally related.

THE RHYTHM OF THE UNI-VERSE

This is an amalgam of the content in the Universe series. It includes verse, supporting text and almost one hundred related full colour illustrations. It presents a unique and interesting introduction to the wonders of the known universe for those who are just developing a burgeoning curiosity in such things.

SNAPSHOTS OF THE UNIVERSE

This is a very much extended and more detailed version of the above publication. The author is aware that having such a subject presented wholly in verse may not be to the liking or satisfy the more inquisitive budding astronomer, physicist or scientist. He realized before finishing the original presentation that a second book was needed to expand in more depth and detail into each poetic subject heading.

Fiction Publications by This Publisher.

Authored by James Duggan.

THE COSMIC MENACE

Earth is faced with total destruction by a threat from outer space which never in the entire history of the planet has been experienced by its inhabitants; neither man nor beast.
Can Pat Buchanan and his strange young associate together with a motley crew of scientists, industrialists and national governments do anything to avoid a total catastrophe?

THE HONEYCOMB BRIEF

If you want a gentle uplifting tale of human endeavour and relationships with a liberal sprinkling of historical and geographical facts plus a huge helping of the 'feel good factor' then read on.

Kate becomes the driving force behind architect James O'Hara's efforts to build a unique National Theme Park. Its purpose is not like that of any other in the world. Finding financial backing for this altruistic project is virtually impossible. In their efforts to raise the necessary funds they are drawn ever closer together, with several other love interests developing amongst the team gathered around them in pursuit of their dream.

As the tale evolves so the pace quickens, with each chapter producing twists and sub plots. There are numerous surprises and seemingly unnatural coincidences emergent from the so called 'Chaos Theory' and the 'Six Degrees of Separation' phenomenon which add to the intrigue.

The author apologises for the tear jerking inclusion of one chapter in particular which cannot fail to moisten the eyes of those readers with a sensitive disposition. However, it was an essential element of the plot and it is hoped it will not spoil your enjoyment of the overall narrative.

Let your own imagination boldly run riot in pursuit of the 'feel good factor'.